21 Windows To Home

Finding Peace Where We All Belong

Arnit (Ayush Saxena)

Made with ❤ on the BookLeaf Publishing Platform
www.bookleafpub.in
www.bookleafpub.com

Dedication

"To those who transform walls into warmth, and spaces into sanctuary"

To my family,

Mom, Arti, whose love is the foundation of every corner,
Dad, Nitin, whose strength and guidance build the pillars
of our home,
And Kushagra, my brother, whose laughter fills the air
with joy.
You are the heartbeats that make our house a home.

This book is for you—my forever place of belonging.

Preface

Preface

For the past eight years, I have lived away from home—first in Chennai during my engineering days, then through a two-year MBA journey in Karjat near Mumbai, and now, as I work in the ever-moving city of Bengaluru. In all that time, my visits home have been fleeting—no more than 20 to 30 days each year. And yet, within those brief windows, I have found a wellspring of strength and solace that carries me through the long stretches of distance and solitude.

This book was born from that realization—the quiet, powerful truth that home is not merely a place, but a feeling etched into the soul by the people who inhabit it. It is a tribute to the quiet heroes who leave behind familiarity, warmth, and laughter, not just in pursuit of ambition, but to craft a legacy of love and security for those they hold dear. These are the people who bear their struggles with grace, who walk through the world with homesick hearts and hopeful eyes.

In these 21 poems, I've tried to distill the essence of

home—not just as a structure, but as a sanctuary; not just as a memory, but as a living, breathing force. This collection is for everyone who knows what it means to carry their home within them—folded in pockets of memory, stitched into daily rituals, and whispered in dreams.

Rumi once wrote,
"Raise your words, not your voice. It is rain that grows flowers, not thunder."
And while his wisdom lingers, I've come to believe something even simpler:
"It's not the walls or the roof that make a home—it's the people, and the love they pour into it".

May these poems remind you of the quiet strength that comes from knowing where you belong—and the enduring warmth of those who wait with open arms.

— **Arnit (A.S.)**

Acknowledgements

Acknowledgements

First and foremost, I offer my deepest gratitude to **God**, whose presence has been a constant source of strength, clarity, and quiet reassurance. In moments of doubt and distance, faith has been my compass—guiding each step and illuminating the path ahead.

I am endlessly thankful to the people who form the heart of my life.

To my mother, **Arti**, whose boundless love is the quiet foundation on which everything rests. To my father, **Nitin**, whose strength, discipline, and steady guidance have shaped my principles and resolve. And to my brother, **Kushagra**, whose laughter and energy bring lightness and joy to every moment. You are my home, my grounding force, and the reason behind every word I write. This book is for you—my forever place of belonging.

I also extend my sincere appreciation to the educators and staff who have played an integral role in my academic and personal development.

To **Campion School, Bhopal**, for laying the foundation of character and curiosity.

To **SRM University, Kattankulathur (Chennai)**, for honing my technical abilities and pushing me to think critically.

To **Universal Business School, Karjat**, and **Cardiff Metropolitan University**, for enriching my understanding of the world and encouraging creative growth.

To every professor, mentor, and member of the support staff—thank you for your commitment, kindness, and the lasting impressions you've left on my journey.

Lastly, to my friends—thank you for your constant encouragement, creative spark, and genuine companionship. Your presence continues to inspire me, both in life and on the page.

To each of you, and to the unseen hands that have helped shape this journey: thank you. This book holds pieces of all of you within it.

— **Arnit (A.S.)**

1. Where the Light Stays On

In the crowd of a distant city,
Between meetings and office walls,
A kid from the 90s, now a man,
Saunters through his memories' halls.

From blackboards and a schoolyard past,
To hostel days where dreams amassed,
A bright light stayed on, with a steady glow,
A beacon calling out his name far from home.

Far away & through rigid grind,
Trained hard, for an ambitious climb,
He kept his home in heart and mind
A place where he felt less confined.

Here are twenty-one windows of his soul,
Each a struggle, each a goal.
Through them shines the light of home,
He's away, but he's never alone.

With the aroma of rain falling on earth's skin,
Those warm cups of cutting chai shared with kin.
These moments of peace were short-lived
As that feeling of being away was still vivid

Even in the modern lands of neon lights,
Where skyscrapers rise to humongous heights,
That light of home remains his guide—
A bright glow that never subsides.

For where the light stays on is a sentiment:
A father's trust, a brother's strength.
A mother's love and lots of prayers
· The light which never wears.

So he writes to bridge the gap between—
The kid he was and all he's seen.
Through 21 windows to his home,
He finds where the light stays on.

Arnit (A.S.)

2. Between Hearth and Hustle

A familiar room, slightly lit,
with the embrace of a soft blanket.
Memories of a lullaby in my mother's voice
An anchor in the rough sea of noise.
A home where I slept & dreamt of warmth,
Of the future in a city filled with charm.

Who knew all that charm was a bait,
I left the comfort for what I dreamt.
I reached & the reality struck me hard,
The city's charm was only a façade.
I left the embrace of my home so mellow,
Lost the sleep to naps so shallow.

Deep in sleep, the future was clear and bright,
But in naps, those dreams dissolved into night.
The blanket is the same, but the room is not,
Without the anchor, my mind distorts.
I wish I had the room, which was slightly lit,

Where deep, unbroken sleep would warmly sit.

As No transient nap could ever mend the night,
I long for that old sleep to make things right.

Arnit (A.S.)

3. Come Home in Rhyme

Come home, if only in these lines,
Let this be the the moment when you realize.
Those moments, you won't live them again,
So cherish home now before you lose them again

The boy you were still waits by that gate,
To pull you inside A world so great
His soft heart beats out home's gentle calm,
Guiding him back to its roots, his healing balm.

Success here glitters in neon and steel,
Yet laughter tastes thin when there's no one to feel;
No pat on the back, No emotions to feel,
Just echoing halls and some friends which heal.

I chose this life as I had dreams,
It's a world that glitters but is so hollow, it seems.
It would be enough If I had some more memories,
Of the joy at home and of those voices that heal.

So I write to the past me, The one who is unaware,
Of the worth of moments, he will miss in this neon glare.
Cherish them deeply—it's a vault with no key,
Where time makes deposits, but never sets them free.

Gather each moment like rare morning dew,
Fragile, fleeting, and forever true.
Let these words nest deeply in your mind,
or you'll pen them again to the child left behind.

Arnit (A.S.)

4. Mango Season in Corporate Towers

I. Arrival

Amidst the tall glass coated towers with polished floors,
A fruit cart appears like a mirage of home.
On mud-cracked ground beneath a yellow umbrella,
Bright mangoes piled, their colors calling forth waves of
nostalgia

II. The Purchase

I swipe my ID card, chasing that beautiful mirage,
A memory of home, A reflection of a beautiful past.
₹100 note in a wrinkled palm exchanges for sunshine
Vendor's knife sings on a yellow sphere with cuts so fine.
Juice beads lie like pearls on my tiffin's lid,
Dripping down—a sweet proof of who once was a kid.

III. First Bite

I retreat to my cubicle in this castle of glass,
walls of muted beige, screens flickering charts.
A yellow peel and a wedge of summer,

The juice is warm, its aroma sweet like sugar
Through bright lights, & AC in a glass dome:
Comes subtly, a molten flash of home.

IV. Reverie

Between meeting calls and email dings,
I taste nostalgia and A rush of feelings
mango-tree shadows folding across time.
Every cube of golden flesh,
feels like reliving those times so divine.

V. Departure

When the last seed lies hollow in my hand,
I press it gently to the glass so grand.
The skyline's ribs of steel stretch far and wide,
A city's heart where dreams and hopes collide.
I hold out summer to these towers tall—
A quiet dare that blooms beyond the wall.

Arnit (A.S.)

5. 2 Sips 1 Chai

At the tapri,
A gust of steam rushes to the face,
Sound chipped cups colliding in trays.
There is no saucer in this world,
here cups rule with stains of tea,
they are colored.

Bustling, steaming, and bitter,
like the city's pulse,
Voices clash over cricket and politics,
& stories of lost love.

Murmur blends in with loud noise,
colleagues sip peace between deadlines.
Their dreams left inside the closed laptops,
They come to taste peace for once,
in theses small chai cups.

Back at home—
oh, the chai experience differs—

A major upgrade to form glass to ceramic cups.
The aroma richer, and this time with the saucer,
A moment so tender,
I wouldn't trade for any other—no bother.

Like the tales my mother once told,
the hollow fritters which I once wore,
That chai was an experience to behold.
For few moments family gathered close,
time slow and sounds of that peaceful slurp,
still echoes.

Here, I chase towers of glass,
count coins under neon sparks.
All strangers holding a steaming cup,
A lone traveler unified by the tapri herd.
The taste of chai at home, a sweet embrace,
It lingers softly, a taste time cannot erase.

The taste of home reminds me,
that the grind is a bridge, not a wall.
between the chai at the tapri and,
the chai at home—we all revolve.
Both brewed from the same leaves,
but steeped in different dreams.

Arnit (A.S.)

6. The Rent is Paid, the Heart is Not

I live in a house where everything is mine,
a fridge humming, and a beautiful windchime
and a window that frames tall glass towers
No leafy trees, no clay pots brimming with water.

The rent is paid, auto-debit, every month,
But the heart...its voice remains unearthed.
I have a rented shelter for which I pay
But my heart still leaves reminders, unpaid.

I own a bed that I alone sleep on,
Nobody to nudge, nobody to lean on.
Sweet Dreams don't knock here
As In this hustle & bustle, they're out of network.

Ma calls every day, never missing a time.
She asks with hope if I'm eating on time.
I lie, like I did about finishing my tiffin-
Some habits linger, without guilt within.

My email storage is cramped.
Still, My room is quiet.
My soul? It is A little scuffed.
Like those whispers, I left behind
the sound of bangles in the kitchen
for the whistle of the 9:00 AM local train.

The rent is paid.
The job is secured.
The pantry is stocked.
But the heart is still in transit,
Hanging like the mist.
between land & sky,
Searching where to sit.

Arnit(A.S.)

7. Festival Flame (A Universal Light)

Diyas light in distant streets,
I light one near, as tradition weaves;
Across the miles, our lights entwine—
One shared feeling, yours and mine.

Echoes of prayers fill my mind,
Festivities, to home, which bind;
Though softer now the festive cheer,
Each diya reminds me we're together.

Beautiful lanterns float in my dreams,
Their paper-thin carrying many dreams;
In distant rooms, I feel their embrace—
A constellation of memories time can't erase.

May every diya we light apart
Bring us closer to each other's hearts;
Miles apart we stand as a family
Wishing to be home even remotely.

Arnit(A.S.)

8. Pocket Shrine

In small pockets of leather kept,
Treasured polaroids softly slept;
No longer drawn for coins or fares,
My wallet's touch still softly cares.

QR Codes have shrunk its role—
A guard of cards, yet some cash, it holds;
Yet in its pockets, lie their memories,
Brimming hopes and sleepless dreams.

Seldom do I glimpse that creased frame,
But whenever I do, the distance shrinks;
Their smiles ignite my courage bright,
Guiding me through lonely nights.

Though dreams lead me away from home,
And yearning shadows sometimes roam,
I relive memories, in one small fold,
And find the courage to be free & bold.

This wallet is not very functional now,
Not to keep money, but just for hope.
This wallet is not very functional now,
Not to keep money, but just for vows.

My pocket shrine, my sacred sign.

Arnit(A.S.)

9. Between the Swipe and the Chime

The morning sun is barely awake,
I swipe my card-the office gate is mine.
A beep, a nod, another day to make,
The city hums, but I feel the time.

Nine A.M., the screen lights up,
Coffee in hand, the world moves on.
But a few times, I'll pack it up,
And head home to where I truly belong.

The flight, the cab, the time fades,
Until the time, I stand outside.
My eyes stunned, memories cascade-
The chime rings and feelings pour inside.

Between the swipe and the chime,
I live two lives, both true, both mine.

Arnit(A.S.)

10. Mom, I'm Busy

Once, the field was my kingdom,
"Mom, I'm playing!"-I'd call from freedom.
I held a Bat in my hands like a sword,
friends around like soldiers who guard.
Her laughter echoed, full of pride,
As her son enjoyed childhood outside.

Now, that kingdom is just a memory,
The sword was replaced by a screens & light.
Still, I say, hurriedly "Mom, I'm busy,",
But this time there's only silence and tube lights.
The ball is lost now, the calls come endlessly,
Meetings replace games packed with delight
.

Yet, in my heart, her voice echoes-
Of belonging, of home, of the life I've made.
From fields to offices, kingdoms have changed,
But Mom's voice remains a constant
So keep your ears open to home,
Kingdoms change but champions don't.

For that voice, don't ever pull out,
As it cheers even from a distant route.

Arnit (A.S.)

11. Circle of Comfort

In the silence of dusk,
I ran down the hall,
He sat by the TV on the sofa,
tiered and grey;
I stood on his feet,
where the day left its toll,
Pressed with young strength,
to bring ease to his soul.

He smiled & said my laughter,
would drive his pain away,
Now towers surround me,
away from him I am today.
My tiered feet ache,
from the miles I have travelled;
Remembering it was you,
now my feet I cradle.

In sunset's orange glow,
at the dawn of the day,

My footsteps recall,
where those memories lay;
From boy into manhood,
I gently make my way,
In a circle of comfort,
A father's embrace.

Arnit(A.S.)

12. Neon Nocturne

City pulses, sapphire glow,
Tower shadows ebb below;
Yet in cups of filter coffee,
I sip the home that lives in me.

Early to bed, early to rise—
Not anymore, not a surprise.
Wide awake during the night,
Sleep vanished in the neon light.

Nights are no longer a time to sleep.
Sometimes I celebrate success with glee,
Or, alone in stress and tears, I weep.
Whether one stays jolly or in grief,
The loss is always that peaceful sleep.

These bright lights and the city's glow
Have made me miss my dreamy pillow.
I know sleepless nights lead to fortune—
Still, these bright lights make you a nocturne.

At home, everyone is asleep,
Dreaming—even if away, he may be at peace.
Hope someday their dreams come true;
May great fortunes come with deep sleep too.

13. A slice of life

Yet whispers of laughter drift through the air,
Each memory cherished, a bond we still share.
Underneath neon skies, where dreams take flight,
I raise a toast to those who still ignite.

With every dance step, their spirits align,
In heartbeats and rhythms, our paths intertwine.
Though distance may stretch, and years may unfold,
Our tales are the treasures, more precious than gold.

So here's to the moments we still hold so dear,
To laughter and love that draw us all near.
In the city that shimmers, with friends by my side,
I send them my love, as the stars start to glide.

Arnit(A.S.)

14. Slam Books and Salary Slips

Under softly lit dawn, he walks his way to the bus stop,
Polished shoes tapping beats on the morning walk;
A flag waves upon us as the anthem echoes in the
assembly hall
In queues, we stand together in neat uniforms from short
to tall

In the canteen line, samosas warm on hot plates,
Friends jostle with laughter beneath a tree's shade;
Two-rupee eclairs, as dessert we split & share,
FlAMES on the last page of a notebook, lovingly made.

Pages of slam books bursting with truths and dares,
Handwritten dreams, a kid enjoying life, unprepared;
Ink-stained words now travel by email, across digital
gates.
Those simple mornings are now reflected in cubicles and
stairs.

Years pass into glass towers where the sun is the same.
He walks through IT parks with card beeps in the lane;
Emails fill the inbox with memories once confined;
The dawn assembly's echo drifts through cubicles all the
time.

Yet in peace and quiet, he still hears childhood calls:
The morning prayer, monsoon football, on the
playgrounds,
A teacher's grin above the chalk-dusted blackboard,
A copy, a pen, daydreams beneath a golden sun.
These memories warm him now through boardroom
calls.

Every pay slip printed holds the past at a glance.
He folds a hopeful smile like origami with his pay-- –
Brisk keystrokes tiptoe on keys, echoing classroom
chance,
He wrote code where once he played with modeling clay.

15. Red Lights Delights

Amidst the modern grey sky,
where smoke prevails clouds subside.
Where even if the road is wide,
there is no place for peace to reside.

The brake lights pulse in silent rows,
faces hidden behind tinted glow.
But beneath the rush, a heartbeat beats,
where community lingers, and kindness greets.

Even the road is built by trust,
The sound "Arre bhai, aao!" drifting through the dust—
hands waving welcome in warm smiles,
inviting hearts to bridge the miles.

Amidst the modern grey sky,
where the chaos and calm collide,
a flicker of warmth, a memory's sigh,
in this tapestry of life, we abide.

Arnit (A.S.)

Arnit (A.S.)

16. Bookshelf Reverie

That sheesham rack in our living room,
Held worlds of words in messy rows:
Dan Brown's Robert Langdon's at the top—
With Some dusty lamps and a ticking clock;
Champak's, Tin tin and Twinkle lie below—
Few treasured show off manga like Naruto.

Dad's Classics, Mom's magazines,
Bent at corners by bedtime dreams;
Malgudi's sunlit lanes and monsoon rains
Flowed through Premchand's beautiful tales.
Between them, slam-book petals remain dry,
Friendship's inked confessions kept sly.

Now in my city flat I stand
Two books only grace my bed:
A poet's murmured lullaby,
A prayer to steady myself.
The rest are PDFs they already slept,
No more the crackle of fresh paper felt,

No holograms for fingers to scratch;

Audiobooks hum through crowded trains,
Their voices rich, but perspective on rent .
I miss the musk of well-worn spines,
The feel of turning pages, so divine.

One day I'll fill a shelf so tall again,
With stories, comics, novels wild and tame.
Until then the shelf stands as a memoir,
It carries the weight till my soul rewires.

Arnit (A.S.)

17. Checklist of Change

I. **Then**

Weekends woke without any alarm bell—
No tasks to tick, no assignments to quell.
We made our "not-to-do" lists in joy:
No alarms, no chores, no rush to employ.
Time drifted like a calm and cool breeze,
Chasing clouds & dreams in the sky with ease.

II. **Now**

Saturday mornings brings a schedule to to:
"1. Gym at eight
2. Grocery run
3. Project draft
4. Call Ma"
Each task holds a promise made—
To bend each minute not to fade.

III. **In Contrast**

Blank paper once meant freedom's tune,
An arti piece born out of a lazy noon.

Today, blank pages feel like a void,
Unchecked boxes now we try to avoid.
We chase the list from dawn to dusk,
Fearing moments left to rust.

IV. **Reflection**

Yet in the soft hush before first light,
A childhood whisper stirs the night:
"Do nothing but breathe today."
I carve one "not-to-do" in gray:
Forget the list—just be awhile,
Let weekend hours return their smile.

Arnit (A.S.)

18. Ticket to happiness

I hold my ticket like that hand,
Which carry's me through this foreign land.
Its paper thin yet very heavy,
with the weight of homebound dreams.

Boarding passes In hands so steady,
Luggage weighed packed and ready.
My heart beats rapidly in boarding zones,.
Leaves signed, and a promise,
to bring a little bit of home ;

Now, all that stands between me and home is sky,
No cloud too distant, no runway too long to pass by.
As in that seat reclines the joy I've carried all along.
Hoping to be home for so long.

Arnit (A.S.)

19. Bow, Blessing, Belonging

I step onto the runway, as I exit the flight,
Wait for the luggage in an endless line,
Wishing for it to come soon at least this time.
I approach the exit sign, with intuition in ny mind,
I see, grown in years yet a familiar sight,
of Dad standing by the car,
Waiting for me with his gentle smile.
My heart races—every suitcase light—
as I cross the distance in long strides,
then bow to touch his weathered feet,
To seel blessing for the child inside me.
His hand rises, On my head his palm lays,
in that blessing, burdens melt away—
A tender calm no triumph can outbid,
In his eyes and arms, I'm ever his kid.,
and at that moment, the home unfolds:
not walls or rooms, but your waiting smile—
an embrace that welcomes me whole.

Arnit (A.S.)

20. Homeward Echoes

I return with tiered hands and reddish eyes,
an innocent soul now shaped by neon skies—
yet nothing cures the silent pain inside
like stepping past that threshold, arms open wide.

Mother's laughter ripples through familiar halls,
lifting my burdens with each gentle call.
Her food's aroma floods my withered core,
a quiet spell that mends me to the floor.

Dad's steady gaze steadies years away,
his proud nod anchoring dreams gone astray.
I feel again the boy beneath that smile—
his blessing recalling every unspoken mile.

Siblings swarm like separated sparrows at dawn,
their playful shrieks brushing sleep until gone.
We race through sunlit lanes of childhood glee,
reclaiming moments time cannot weave.

By evening's quiet, we sit in woven light,
sharing my city tales into the night—
their "Waah, beta!" lifting my doubts like wings,
reminding me what home's true treasure brings.

Each laugh, each tear, each familiar embrace
becomes a lamp no skyline can replace.
When office calls bid me once more I depart,
I'll carry this refuge sealed within my heart.

And you, who wander far from where you started,
may these words stir that kid sleeping in your heart—
for though we chase horizons bright and wide,
home's gentle song forever calls us inside.

Arnit (A.S.)

21. The Window To Home

Across these pages—twenty poems deep—
I've traced your footsteps, to your home so sweet,
Awaken the kid you tucked beneath deadlines and sleep,
And lit through ink that gentle, whispered poems plea.

Remember those hands you once held tight?
The ones you held & raced under sunlight—
They wait in voices soft as morning dew,
In laughter, tears, and everyday talks about you.

So pause your rush. Pick up the phone tonight,
Call home, let your stories weave their smile.
Let "How are you?" bloom into shared delight,
And ask, "What dream shall we chase, from tonight."

Video-call their smiles; gift them bits of joy—
A packet of treats, a book you together enjoyed,
A single flower plucked for your dear ones,
A token that proclaims, "You're all I need.", for once.

Send laughter in a text, or mail a note,
For every small surprise revives the heart.
In these gentle threads, our love is kept afloat—
A tether that no distance can depart.

The child inside you still reaches for hand,
That welcomes you with warmth no time can fade.
So wrap them in your care, here tiptoe and stand—
And let this poem be the promise made:

To never let those hands feel out of reach,
To hold them close with every word and deed,
For home lives in these moments we beseech—
And in this love, we plant our lasting seed.

Arnit (A.S.)

www.ingramcontent.com/pod-product-compliance
Lightning Source LLC
Chambersburg PA
CBHW061724130726

47996CB00006B/2494